DESIGNING INFIDELITY

A Reference Guide to
the Art of Cheating to Perfection

BY

J. FRANCES

authorHOUSE™

1663 Liberty Drive, Suite 200
Bloomington, Indiana 47403
(800) 839-8640
www.AuthorHouse.com

First published by AuthorHouse 2/10/2006

ISBN: 1-4208-9644-X (e)
SBN: 1-4208-9643-1 (sc)

Library of Congress Control Number: 2005909755

Printed in the United States of America
Bloomington, Indiana

This book is printed on acid-free paper.

CONTENTS

Introduction   xiii

Chapter 1
Strategy ... Sounds Like a Plan   2

Chapter 2
Suspecting vs. Unsuspecting ... Who's on
First?   12

Chapter 3
Home Phones/Cell Phones ... Sorry, Wrong
Number   20

Chapter 4
Email ... Never Put Anything in Writing   30

Chapter 5
Credit Cards ... Pick a Card, Any Card!   40

Chapter 6
Hotels vs. Motels ... I'd Like to Make a
Reservation   48

Chapter 7
Overnight Excursions ... Wishful Thinking   54

Chapter 8
Public Places ... Do We Dare?   64

Chapter 9
Timing/Scheduling ... Ticktock, Ticktock   72

Chapter 10

    Internet Affairs ... Click, Double Click   82

Chapter 11

    Lust vs. Love ... When the Smoke Clears   88

Epilogue   95

RULE #1

Suspicion creates doubt...Discreet reading required!

... for Pumpkinhead and Pooknut

INTRODUCTION

Affairs are like snowflakes; no two are the same ... nor do they last forever.

Having an affair is not rocket science; it's merely a matter of the heart, your heart.

There is no justifying an affair in the eyes of our traditionalized society or in the eyes of your partner. You are the only one who can justify infidelity in your marriage or relationship. Your reasons are what they are, be it mental or physical stimulation, midlife crisis, the need for rockets' red glare, desire, lust, passion, intrigue, mystery, sexual addiction, or an entirely different reason. Your affair is your own.

If you are casually or seriously contemplating having an affair or already involved in one, there are a considerable number of ways to cover those proverbial tracks.

It is this author's opinion that nothing is foolproof or guaranteed. We can only be as careful as we can so that we don't get caught and no one gets hurt.

The next few chapters outline the do's and don'ts and in no way condemn or condone the reasons for your affair. Whatever has led you down this road, you're here, so proceed with caution.

CHAPTER 1

STRATEGY ...
SOUNDS LIKE A PLAN

When we talk about strategy, infidelity and betrayal don't usually top the list as one of our best laid-out plans. Even the worst of plans require thought, regardless of the outcome.

There is no specific set of rules or guidelines to follow when it comes to deception and betrayal, but caution, details, and your partner's unawareness require your full and immediate consideration at all times. These key elements, always at the forefront, will allow us to plan ahead accordingly.

Comfort level—Never find a comfort level in your affair. We try to get away with something once, twice, and we get comfortable. What happens when we get comfortable? We get sloppy.

Lovers—Choose your potential lover wisely. We don't always have control over with whom we find attractive and feel the chemistry. Some of us (believe it or not) aren't even aware that someone other than our partner has now sparked our interest and is consuming our every thought. I call this the "subconscious awareness" state of infidelity.

We sense the needs that have gone astray; but aren't consciously looking to betray our partners. Whatever our conscious or subconscious state may be, we must become aware of one very important fact; it is absolutely imperative not to get involved with someone who is unattached. A single person has nothing to lose, and we all know about hell having no fury (male or female). This is a perfect example of opening up Pandora's Box. Choose a lover who is just as committed as you. Should your affair last a week or a year, it has to end on a mutual note.

One-night stand—Never assume that a one-night stand may be the way to go if your reasons for infidelity are purely for sexual fulfillment. A one-night stand can be more dangerous than finding a lover with mutual considerations. This scenario is good for the business traveler who has the odds in his or her favor; however, it is very important to know with whom you are getting into bed, even for just one night. No one should be exempt from causing you a problem, no matter the distance or circumstance. A one-night stand is still a form of infidelity and can be just as damaging for you and your partner if discovered.

Trust—It is very difficult to have an affair without having someone you can trust almost as much as yourself. We all need someone who can and will vouch for our whereabouts when we are manipulating time with our lovers. This should only be limited to very trustworthy friends or co-workers—people you can trust implicitly and, no matter what disagreements you may encounter, will remain true to your friendship. In this genre, it is important to have reliable alibis. If you are planning to spend a substantial amount of time with your lover, you cannot depend on the small excuses that only allow you an hour or two. Don't use the same friends on a consistent basis; always mix it up so that a pattern is not formed or obvious to your partner.

Explanations—I think most of us who are engaged in infidelity can write a book or two when it comes to the excuses and lies used to coordinate our affairs. Never leave anything to probability! A well-thought-out excuse combined with truth will always hold up better than a last-minute excuse. Always assume that your partner has suspicions of your whereabouts when you are with your lover. Have your reasons for being late or unreachable ready when you finally arrive home. A well-rehearsed answer will allow you the leverage for direct eye contact and a smooth flow of words without hesitation.

Calling your partner right after leaving your lover is also important; it will give you some insight to his or her attitude or something unsettling in his or her voice. Should your partner suspect something, you can proceed with your excuse via telephone before you arrive home. It's extremely important for your partner to believe your excuses when absent from home.

Awareness—Don't ever lose sight of reality! We must stay in sync with our own awareness when it comes to ourselves. In every book or article that I've read on infidelity and betrayal, there is always one section that talks about the signs of infidelity and the changes we as individuals go through once we travel down this road. We may not be aware of the physical or mental changes that take place, but our partners are very much aware—a difference in our body language, attention, weight, appearance, demeanor, etc. We are so in tune with our newfound libidos that we don't realize the obvious metamorphosis taking place.

- ♦ Don't change anything; focus on everything remaining the same at home, especially sex. If you are still having sex with your partner, then you need to continue the routine no matter how ungratifying it may now feel.
- ♦ Change your clothes outside of home when meeting your lover; an obvious change in

the way you look, especially if it's sudden, is one of the first signs of infidelity.

♦ If you feel the need to self-improve for your lover, then try to use a bit of reverse psychology in leading your partner to suggest you try something new to improve upon your appearance. Make it known to your partner how discontented you are about yourself and plant the power of suggestion. Let your partner suggest that change is good for you.

♦ Be aware of the old habits that you just can't break and don't try to break them. Gradually change the habits you can. It's important that you keep your partner off balance. Be unpredictable in nature and not an open book.

Time manipulation—Without question, the favorite excuse for finding time to be with your lover (while not involving trustworthy friends) is the "sidetrack excuse".

♦ This involves a phone call to your partner during the course of the workday explaining that you have some errands to run after work. Go on to explain exactly what they are. By the time you arrive home, and before your partner can ask any questions, proceed to explain that you never made it to A, B, or C because you got sidetracked with D, E, and F. This excuse eliminates doubt in your partner, puts you in a place that you didn't need to explain or prove previously, and explains why you weren't where you said you were going, just in case your partner was trying to check.

♦ Using overtime as an excuse is acceptable if you can produce the additional income and if your partner doesn't try to check up on you. Most of us cannot add income to our paychecks. Cash works; borrow it. Salaried employees don't collect overtime unless they're non-exempt. Use the excuse that works for you or don't use it!

♦ Never pick a fight with your partner (over trivial or important issues) to create a reason for leaving the house without an explanation.

♦ Do not accuse your partner of cheating to take the spotlight off yourself; the guilty are usually the accusers.

♦ Always leave your cell phone in the car during rendezvous, as this should be your explanation for not answering. This also follows the rules of advice in adding some truth to the numerous lies. However, if you are one of those people who constantly wear their cell phone on their person, then this excuse will indicate a change in your normal habits.

If some or all of this chapter has planted the seed of doubt before you find yourself involved in lust and betrayal, then you may move on to the next chapters.

Constant doubt in self-judgment will keep you on your toes and in bed with your lover.

CHAPTER 2

SUSPECTING VS. UNSUSPECTING ... WHO'S ON FIRST?

Never underestimate the knowledge of your partner.

We would all like to think that we know our partners better than they know themselves. This would ultimately put us in a better place when it comes to "cover" stories. Only you know what your partner would accept as a probable excuse for your absence while having an affair.

Suffice it to say, lying unfortunately plays an integral part in covering for your time and must be believable by your partner's standards. If your partner is unsuspecting, then you have the leverage needed to alter the truth and spend time with your lover without additional anxiety. It is the nature of the beast to be unsuspicious at first, never to think our partners would betray us. It is also a natural instinct, or a "safe mode," not to believe the truth when it comes to infidelity. When our perfect worlds become threatened, the denial factor takes hold, and we want to believe the lie over the truth in order to protect what's ours. Once the trust factor is destroyed, it's almost impossible to regain. Individually, we think we'll never be the one to get caught. Whether we plan to have an affair or it just happens, we still take the plunge.

"One lie leads to a hundred" may be one of the most common phrases used today, but it holds more truth than the lie itself. It sometimes amazes me how one small white lie can start out and gain the momentum of a domino effect. Before we know it, our conversation with our partner now consists of a dozen or more lies. How do we remember what we've told our partners? Is it realistic to think that we don't have to remember the lies after we've told them? These scenarios somehow find their way back to us, and we must be prepared. The irony of our lies is that our partners remember them better than we do. It's the truth that makes its way to our memory banks; the lies have a way of leaving our bodies once they're spoken.

Even if you consider yourself to be a good, believable liar, don't take any chances in forgetting the important details of the lies used to open up the time you've spent with your lover. If possible, make a private journal entry (unattainable) marking the date and brief description of what you told your partner. This may sound contradictory to *"never put it in writing,"* but there is always one exception to every rule, especially when it comes to remembering where we were "supposed to be" and with whom.

Use this journal just like the textbook you would use if studying for an important exam. Try to memorize all or most of the facts. This should be done on a weekly or monthly basis, depending on how often you spend time with your lover. Once embedded in our brain, we can quickly remember what we used as a feasible excuse should our whereabouts of the night in question resurface.

Maria, a thirty-one-year-old medical receptionist from Cincinnati, Ohio, describes an unprepared confrontation in front of her spouse.

"I was so proud of myself when I was able to manipulate four hours away from home to have dinner and sex with my lover. My husband didn't suspect a thing. I had explained that I was going to have dinner with an old friend who was in town and, without hesitation, invited my husband to join us. Praying he would say no and not want to participate in a 'girls' night out, it was necessary to extend the invitation in order to provide my husband with the comfort I needed him to feel. I was also prepared to make a three-way conference call to my good friend just in case my husband decided to call my cell phone to say hello."

*"Several weeks later while shopping with my husband at a nearby mall, I bumped into a friend of mine who innocently asked me if I had seen our **mutual** 'old' friend. Not being the studious person I should have been in remembering my lies, I quickly responded with the truth which was 'no', 'I haven't seen her in a while.' Needless to say from the look on my husband's face, he quickly became suspecting of the night in question. What happened to dinner?"*

"I was now in a position to explain why I had lied with yet another lie and no time to think about what to say. Twenty lies later, I managed to escape the mistaken truth I told in front of my husband ... I was planning a surprise for him and needed a cover ... end of story. Now all I needed was the surprise."

What do you do when your spouse suspects that "something is rotten in the state of Denmark" and isn't quoting Shakespeare?

A suspecting partner has many good reasons to become suspecting, especially when an out-of-the-ordinary situation or circumstance leads your partner into this category. Suspicion comes from change. Has your personality, demeanor, or simply your daily habits changed as a result of your newfound affair? Some partners may be oblivious to change, and others are very much aware. Be prepared for a lot of additional questions and phone calls, and, if taken to the extreme, the possibility of being followed by your partner or someone known to your partner.

If you weren't caught "with your pants down", so to speak, there may be ways to alleviate the suspicion your partner carries. It's very hard to push the antennas down once they're up, but not impossible. The most important thing to do is try to rebuild the trust factor.

SUGGESTIONS:

- ♦ Reduce the obvious time spent with your lover.
- ♦ Flip your time after work into the course of the workday. Your partner is less likely to suspect any extracurricular activities while you are supposed to be working.
- ♦ If your partner is employed, manipulate the time during your partner's workday.
- ♦ Don't change the patterns that obviously made your partner suspicious. Mix it up so that you can't be bound to consistency.

- Don't reduce time spent away from home, but don't increase it either.
- Be exactly where you say you are going and with the person(s) you are meeting.
- Always answer your cell phone. When a suspicious partner can't get you on your cell phone for any length of time, the antennas go up and you become accountable for your whereabouts.

Regaining your partner's trust begins with a double dose of truth before injecting any more lies.

CHAPTER 3

HOME PHONES/CELL PHONES ... SORRY, WRONG NUMBER

Wasn't that a movie? Even wrong numbers are hard to explain if they happen frequently enough. Hang-ups are much worse. Whether you have a suspecting or unsuspecting partner, never, ever, give out your home number. It's all about taking chances again. Sometimes when we're home alone, we seize the opportunity to make a quick call to our lovers using the home phone. Is your phone number listed? If so, only ET should be phoning home.

Does your lover live out of the area? The dialed number will then appear on your telephone bill. Unless you've done your investigative homework on whether this may or may not be a local call, restrict yourself from using your home phone. If you **must** call from home, another option is to purchase a calling card; the dialed number will not show up on your bill. Lastly, let's not forget the redial button; this is another surefire way of having to explain an unexplainable phone call. Delete the call log or last number dialed immediately after your call to your lover.

Today's technology is a real hindrance when it comes to betrayal. The caller ID box identifies the name, number, date, and time of an incoming call. Does your lover have caller ID on his or her home or cell phone? If so, he or she can immediately see what number you are calling from and make a permanent record. Unlist your home number or dial *67 per call; this way it will show up as unavailable or private on a caller ID box or cell phone. If your home number is presently published in the phone book, then there's no need to worry about caller ID. Do you trust your lover? That's another chapter.

CELL PHONES

They say, "A bird in hand is worth two in the bush." Not in the case of cell phones. Make sure you have two. They should be identical to one another (if possible) just in case you accidentally leave it in plain view. One should be the family cell phone. Feel free to leave this phone around the house, and on occasion, ask your partner to answer a call for you and also ask him or her to retrieve voicemail with your password. This will give your partner a definite comfort level.

The other cell phone should be private, so private that only you and your lover know of its existence. Your private cell phone should be your main source of communication between you and your lover and should be used most cautiously when at home.

Did I say it was okay to call your lover from home? That's your "call," but yes, **Howard, a fifty-five**

year-old stockbroker from Chicago, has done it on many occasions.

"When I'm home, I keep my eyes peeled on the view of the street in anticipation of visitors. I've even ventured to call when my wife was at home. Again, making sure I wasn't within ear-shot distance, hiding in a room or closet with the door cracked so I could see anyone coming."

When making a call like that, it should be a quick voicemail using the "back door" number directly into your lover's voicemail on his or her cell phone. Many cellular services have a "back door" number, which allows you to bypass a live call and leave a direct voicemail message. Common sense should tell us that a live conversation with your lover is not an option while your partner is at home. Suppose your lover's phone is on when you call, what do you say? "Hi, I can't talk right now; just wanted to let you know I was thinking about you," click! Avoid the reminder of the spouse's presence and utilize direct voicemail.

THINGS TO REMEMBER

- Don't chance a live conversation from home, especially when you're not alone.
- Text messaging is a safer and easier option to use when at home, just as long as you remember to erase your in/outbox.

♦ Remember to hide your private cell phone when at home and always take it with you.

♦ Have the bill sent to your office or P.O. box.

♦ If you are apprehensive about having an additional cell phone in your name or having the bill come to your office, I suggest a pay-as-you-go cell phone. These phones can be bought in most electronic stores, and some newer vehicles also offer a built-in phone with the pre-purchase of minutes. Be careful with what you use to buy these minutes. Refer to Chapter 5 on credit cards.

♦ Another option is to have a trustworthy friend apply for a cell phone in his or her name and **YOU** pay the bill.

♦ Always erase from your private cell phone all call logs, recent calls, dialed calls, and received calls. Do not store any numbers in speed dial.

♦ After listening to your lover's voicemail, erase it (no souvenirs allowed).

♦ A flip-type phone is the phone of choice; it protects the keypad from the redial and speed-dial features. It also saves time in locking and unlocking the keypad.

♦ Be wary of the cell phones that take digital pictures. You may think someone is dialing a number when he or she could actually be taking your picture.

Keep in mind that our partners who may be suspecting may also be very resourceful in finding out information through your cellular carriers and can easily find your recent call log without having access to the paper bill. Most cellular Internet sites offer a detailed report on unbilled usage; all that's required is some personal information to log on to the site. This is why a second cell phone is a safety feature for your marriage or relationship and a communication requirement for your affair.

Regarding safety features, **Gina, a thirty-eight-year-old sales manager from Buffalo, New York, describes how she got caught red-handed using her cell phone.**

"Well, actually, I wasn't using it at all, but I had my phone in the on position one day when my lover came to meet me. In leaning over to share a kiss hello, my cell phone pressed up against the shift in my car and either speed dialed or redialed the number to my home. Ouch! (A private cell phone with a flip cover would have come in very handy right about then.) Needless to say, my husband

answered the call only to hear my familiar voice engaged in a warm conversation with someone else. There was no getting out of this one, no dancing. It was plain and simple; I had to admit to something. When the connection was lost, my spouse returned the call to my cell phone and told me what he had heard. I replied with, 'I'll be right home, and we'll discuss it.' The car ride home gave me ample time to think."

"It was simple, the only thing to do was confess to the obvious conversation and let the truth be told. I immediately explained to my husband that my reason for 'deceit' was due to unhappiness in our marriage. I made clear the real reasons for what I lacked at home to impulsively look elsewhere. Vulnerability and the desperate need for time and attention brought me to this place."

"This wasn't a well-accepted excuse but the only one that my husband could come to terms with, because it was the truth. If I wanted to end my marriage abruptly, this would have been the opportune time to do so. However, the reason for calling it an affair is because I had decided to remain married. A divorce wasn't in the cards, nor was losing my husband over the speed-dial feature."

Gina's then-unsuspecting spouse had now become a member of the "SSS" (Suspecting Spousal Society), and the "trust" factor that gave her ample time with her lover was now gone.

Gina's affair now stood the test of time, but she did end up with another cell phone.

CHAPTER 4

EMAIL ... NEVER PUT ANYTHING IN WRITING

It seems simple enough: a few typed sentences, a click of the mouse, and instant communication with your lover. It's the computer age; the main source of communication for business and pleasure is done through email. Have you ever wondered how the email you've sent is being used on the recipient's end? Email could be saved, printed, or forwarded with history.

Email to your lover is probably the second-most-used source of communication outside of cell phones, and it should be used wisely. There are many Internet providers that offer free email accounts. You can have one or ten; just don't let your partner know of their existence. Again, as I explained in Chapter 3 (on cell phones), allow your partner to check your primary email account frequently. It's all about having your partner feel a certain comfort level, which will in turn allow you the freedom to manipulate the time spent with your lover. The trust factor is very important to maintain as a constant between your partner and you.

If you have a partner who is just as computer literate as you, then you need to keep a constant focus on what you would do if you wanted to read your partner's email. It would be great if your partner didn't know how to turn on a computer, but don't be fooled by ignorance; it's no excuse for the law and should be no excuse for you. There's always someone somewhere willing to teach us something and the adventurous kind who teach themselves.

As much as some of us would like to think we're incurable romantics and could express it better in writing, save those love letters and stick to the basics. How would you explain an email that was printed, forwarded, or mailed to your partner with all those (sexual) terms of endearment or meeting plans? Ever hear of a disgruntled employee? How about a disgruntled lover? Not every affair ends on an amicable note.

Maryann, a forty-eight-year-old nurse from West Palm Beach, Florida, used to print out almost every piece of email her lover sent her. If she didn't print it, she saved it on her computer.

"The words were beautiful and better expressed in emails than in person, but I knew I had to delete them on my PC, and having a paper trail was proof of the affair, so I followed in Oliver North's footsteps and bought a shredder."

"Gratefully, I have no horror stories of getting caught via email. My partner (to my knowledge) is computer illiterate, but I still take no chances with my email accounts. I leave my primary email account with password (sans any love connections) open all day on my home computer for all to see."

Again, it's about trying to prove you have nothing to hide. Suspicion creates doubt, and spousal comfort allows more time with your lover.

I do have a friend whose affair got deleted because she didn't delete!

Patty, a forty-nine-year-old financial analyst from Rye, New York, was sharing the excitement of her newfound lover (with sexual details included) to a trustworthy friend via email. Incisively enough, Patty deleted her sent mail so as to not leave any details of her torrid affair behind, but what she didn't anticipate was her friend responding to her email with history attached. Needless to say, this email was discovered and read by her then-unsuspecting husband. Have you ever wanted to put the milk back into the carton?

As one of the newest members of the "SSS," he routinely reviewed the history of the Internet sites that were visited by their home shared computer. Noticing that hotmail.com was just visited and frequently, her husband decided to visit the site to see what he could discover. Storing her user ID and password didn't make my friend the sharpest knife in the drawer, but not being as computer literate as her husband provided him with the edge that Patty didn't possess. She was clueless to the fact that Internet Explorer allowed her husband to view the sites she recently visited.

I myself am not an MIS expert, but knowing that there are a lot more advanced techniques for uncovering information, I decided to enlist the help of a professional who certainly opened a few "zip" files we need to view.

1. Please familiarize yourself with the new spyware software; it captures your keystrokes. This could easily be installed by your partner and put you in a very vulnerable position. Regularly check your system for spyware! You can use Spybot or Ad-Aware for free, or purchase another spy blocker system. Remember to keep the software updated and run it at least once a week if not every time you use your computer.

2. Watch out for keystroke-capture hardware. These are tiny hardware devices that are attached to your system between the CPU and the keyboard. They can keep a record of all the keystrokes that you type.

3. Get a personal firewall! If you connect your computer to a network, your computer can be scanned without your knowledge. The spy software that is looking at your machine is not on the computer so it will not be detected. A properly configured firewall will not allow any other computer to look at your system. Read the setup information closely and follow the manufacturer's instructions.

4. Secure passwords. Most people use the same three or four passwords for everything. This is a mistake! Having the perfect system with an easy password is as good as taking no precaution at all. Use a password that you have never used before. A good method is the song code. Take a song that you like and use the first letter in each word of the first line. If you like the song "Raindrops Keep Falling on My Head," your password could be RKFOMH and add a number like your current age or date.

5. Finally, make sure you remove all the temporary files and cookies from your computer. The best way to do this is by using a third-party software. You want to get something that will empty the recycle bin; clear recent documents, recent URLs, and run history; and delete Internet Explorer cookies, Internet Explorer history, your temporary files, and Internet Explorer temporary Internet files. Make sure that you can customize it so that you can choose what to save and what to erase.

6. If you want to skip all this cloak and dagger stuff, use an Internet café. Let them handle the security for you. It is not a 100 percent guarantee that you will not be followed and observed, but you are assured that it will be very hard for someone to get information off the system that you are using. Besides, it's much easier to dance around an explanation for your visit to an Internet café than an email from your lover.

The above information is all from an MIS expert; however, I do have a few suggestions from research and experiences:

♦ Never send or retrieve email from a home-based computer unless it's your own portable laptop or notepad. This eliminates all that worry about spyware, firewalls, hardware devices, etc.

♦ As added security, password-protect your personal laptop or notepad from the user log-on (bios) screen.

♦ Patty now uses her computer at work and never at home. It helps her sleep at night; but be aware that you can easily be monitored in some way by the technology services department, depending on the size of your company. Check to see what rules are in place regarding allowed and banned sites. As long as you are discreet and do not abuse the system, this may be within acceptable limits.

♦ Never use a name that can be remotely linked back to you. Use alphanumeric characters in your user ID.

♦ Change your password like your under-wear.

♦ Delete, delete, and delete! Never save a received email and always delete your sent mail.

- Use assumed names and fictitious information when applying for your email accounts.
- Never forward an email from your lover to anyone.
- Do not send your lover an instant message should you see him or her online from your buddy list; suppose it's someone else?
- When replying, do not reply with history and leave off your John Hancock.
- Last but not least, tell your trusted friends about your affairs in person and not via email!

CHAPTER 5

CREDIT CARDS ...
PICK A CARD, ANY CARD!

It might have worked for Rodney Dangerfield in *Easy Money*, but will it work for you? Wouldn't it be grand if we could write our lives like a movie script?

The use of credit cards in an affair with our lovers is a very functional instrument. It's also a tangible way of getting caught. A simple piece of paper called a receipt, if unexplainable, can and will cause a fair amount of suspicion between you and your partner. Some of us may be able to dance around the reason for a credit card receipt if accidentally found. The businessperson, for example, can always claim "entertainment purposes" as an acceptable excuse, but we don't all fall into this category.

Speaking of categories, **Tom, a fifty-six-year-old plumber from Fairfield, CT,** accidentally stuffed a credit card receipt in his coat pocket.

"In leaving a restaurant one night, the distraction of being with my lover and in a public place gave me a severe bout of bad judgment. I forgot to throw away the receipt from dinner."

"It wouldn't have been so terrible if I used the closet to hang my coat instead of tossing it over a chair in the living room for my wife to collect."

"I was at work the next morning when my wife called me and casually asked me where I had dinner the evening prior. Having spent so many hours away from home as well as quite a distance away, put me in an explicable situation."

Why is it that you never have the time to think of a logical explanation, at least one your partner will accept, when you need it fast? This is why I preach, "Have an answer ready before the question is proposed!"

An emergency call and then dinner at a nearby restaurant was all Tom could produce on the spur of the moment. His lie became the truth when he said he needed to "snake" a customer's pipes. Tom held true to his profession.

Figuring out the logistics of having an affair is hard enough without the additional worry of all the details. In addition to the credit card receipt or chit, we also need to give a considerable amount of thought to the credit card and the statement.

Throwing away the receipt seems simple enough, get rid of the evidence, but that's only the beginning. The credit card statement, which obviously has to go somewhere, must be given considerable attention.

There are several options for obtaining and using credit cards:

♦ Obtain a P.O. box for your credit card statements. This may seem inconvenient to some, but looking at the bigger picture, it could be quite a convenience for not getting caught. A small P.O. box is a nominal fee per month or year, some under $100. You will need to apply for it in your name or the name of a trustworthy friend, as a valid driver's license is required for the rental.

♦ Sending your statements to your office may be another option or risk, if you will, as long as you have a comfort zone. How many hands does the mail go through before it actually reaches your desk? Can it be opened accidentally? Do you need anyone to know that you receive personal mail at work versus home? Why put yourself in a position to have to explain anything to a co-worker?

♦ Another new and interesting way of receiving credit card statements is through e-bill. Most banks and credit card companies now offer sending you your statement via your email. Have it sent to your "private" email account. This will obviously eliminate paper statements. Before opting for this option, be clear on Chapter 4 on email.

My last suggestion is potentially ideal if you have a close friend you trust unconditionally. Ask your friend to apply for a credit card and add you to the account as an authorized user. As an authorized user, you have no contractual responsibility for this account, and it minimizes the chances of your partner discovering a credit card or the statements. The statements would obviously be mailed to your friend's address of choice, and your only concern is to pay the bill.

If you don't have a trusted friend, then you will need to discreetly apply for a credit card unknown to your partner. This brings up another potential problem. Does your partner have access to your credit report? This tell-all report will give a detailed list of the creditor, date it was opened, balance, individual account, and the "address" of application.

Using a credit card that "swipes in the family" is forbidden and will put you in a very precarious situation with your partner.

Please note: Use cash whenever possible. This is not always an option, especially when it comes to hotels; however, it is virtually risk free.

Covering your own credit card bases can still put you at a big disadvantage if your lover hasn't taken the same secure steps. If your lover picks up the tab, be sure to question the security of the credit card in question.

Your lover may be quick to admit to your identity if put in an exposed situation with his or her partner.

CHAPTER 6

Hotels vs. Motels …
I'd Like to Make a
Reservation

Wouldn't it be grand if the "no-tell hotel" existed? The line for timeshares would be around the corner!

It's all about taking chances again. It may not be so wise to make reservations under your own name or the name of your lover. It's one of the many perils in having an affair.

What other choices do we have? There aren't many when it comes to hotels. As we all know, a reservation requires a guarantee and payment with a credit card. So even if you make the reservation using an assumed name, your credit card will reflect your real name. You can use cash upon check-in in most hotels; however, they will require a fair amount of information along with a photocopy of your driver's license. Just what we need, our name and photo in lights.

If you have a trustworthy friend (preferably single), you can ask to use his or her name and credit card. If you are part of the corporate society, you can also make a reservation in your company's name, and if you have a company credit card, use it and reimburse the company for personal use. This scenario obviously applies to only a select few.

Roger, a thirty-eight-year-old restaurant owner in New York City, has on many occasions made reservations at hotels that range from two stars to five stars using his real name and credit card. He obviously uses a credit card that is unknown to his partner and a P.O. box for the statements.

My recommendation, should you decide to follow in Roger's footsteps, is to move around among different hotels. Do not frequent any one hotel in particular, even if you find a comfort level with one. You don't need to be on a first-name basis with the hotel manager or bellhop.

Driving a distance is recommended if you have the time. Are you a gambler? This is about odds. Odds are in your favor if you check into a hotel that is not in your town, or state; however, you do need to make additional time for travel. This is where we get sloppy because proximity and convenience are always important issues between you and your lover. A convenient place to meet means more time spent with one another, not more travel time. You need to weigh the pros and cons in certain instances: more time in bed or going the extra mile to reduce your chances of someone seeing you? Bumping into a frienemy (friendly enemy) in a hotel lobby is extremely difficult if not impossible to explain.

Dining at the restaurant or bar in the hotel is certainly not on the top-ten list of things to do unless you want to get caught. I certainly recommend room service; if the hotel is a "no frills" hotel, bring your own.

Although the "no-tell" motel doesn't actually exist, there are certainly many "no-frills" motels. Here you can pay cash up front and use an assumed name, and some even provide an hourly rate. The amenities include a courtesy phone call from the motel clerk when your time is up, but that's it! Whatever your standards are for luxury, you and your lover will have to compromise for safekeeping and not housekeeping.

These motels are probably the most common type of meeting place for a clandestine affair, and the most information they require is a name and the plate number from your vehicle. Of course you can be identified through your license plate, but this type of establishment's clients are comprised of lovers from all walks. The turnaround of people is so vast that the motel clerk would need a photographic mind to remember everyone who checked in on an hourly rate.

Again, I don't recommend frequenting one hotel or motel in particular, especially on a regular basis.

CHAPTER 7

Overnight Excursions ...
Wishful Thinking

Star light, star bright, "can I please sleep in the arms of my lover for just one night"? It goes back to that old adage of always wanting more. When is enough, enough?

We spend more time yearning for more time with our lovers. The hours we do have to spend are few and far between, and the want and desire to stay a minute longer can be overwhelming. Has your mind ever wandered to thoughts of going to sleep and waking up in the arms of your lover with everything else that falls in between? You wouldn't be normal if you didn't, but thinking it and actually doing it are two different things.

There are three drawbacks to an overnight excursion, one with your partner, one with your lover, and one with yourself. The obvious is your partner uncovering your disloyalty. The second and third drawbacks have nothing to do with getting caught; they have to do with you and your lover. Most people in affairs don't focus on the negative aspects of sharing something so exciting with their lover. "You can't miss something you've never had." Well, now that you've had it, that wonderful overnight blissful experience that you could only fantasize about, what do you do? A fantasy has now become a reality. Will the memory of that time be enough, or will you want more?

Should you choose to journey into the night ...

- ♦ A plan between you and your lover must be meticulously planned.
- ♦ You must give careful consideration to the story line that you create to make your great escape.
- ♦ You and your lover must be in sync with the smallest of details together. What he doesn't think of, she will, and vice versa. All bases must be covered.
- ♦ Your main focus must be on your strategy. Strategy is the single most important element in spending the night together. It must be well structured and premeditated, leaving no stone unturned . It has to be believable to your partner and, to some degree, provable.
- ♦ Planning a business trip? That may be fine for you, but how will your lover meet up with you, and what excuse will he or she use? Can your lover plan a business trip or otherwise at the same time? Will your partner confirm the business trip with your office?

The percentage of affairs in the workplace is high, but the risks involved are higher. What will your co-workers think if you are both out of the office at the same time? Is it just coincidence that you both went on the same business trip together or took the same days off? Can you afford to have the potential office gossip make its way back to your partner?

What about a weekend away from your partner and family? Do you have a believable explanation for going away for a night or two? A bachelor party perhaps? Only you know what your partner will accept and moreover believe in your absence. There must be some truth combined with your lies.

Sending yourself an invitation to an overnight event might work, but this requires planning on your part and trustworthy friends who are willing to confirm and cover for you.

Carissa, a forty-two-year-old mother of three from Orlando, Florida, was kind enough to share the details of her well-planned overnight adventure with her lover.

"Three years into our affair, my lover and I decided it was time we plan to spend a night together. At first it seemed impossible, something we could

only talk about but never really put into motion, until one day I decided to take the next step and test the waters at home before going swimming."

"I reminisce over the card store where I bought a package of bridal shower invitations. I filled out one of the invitations, disguising my handwriting, and mailed it to my attention at home. Luckily, a friend of mine had just moved out of state and was planning to marry in the upcoming year, so a bridal shower was imminent. I would ask my husband to accompany me on this short, boring trip in hopes of his decline. The plan was to meet out of state and stay at a discreet resort."

"I saw this as the perfect opportunity, as well as a great cover story, to invite some friends that would accompany me on this trip—friends who were trustworthy, very much aware of the details of my affair, and extremely open to the suggestion of spending a couple of days at a resort town. Leaving home with friends in tow validated the passage. My plan was to spend two days with them, living up to the truth of my excursion, and the last day and night with my lover."

"My lover met me at the hotel; I was waiting for him in the lounge. I remember how I felt when I saw him, like a schoolgirl; nothing else mattered;

it all felt so right for one day. The night we spent together was everything I thought it would be and more; sometimes I wish it were the worst night of my life."

"We all left the hotel together the next day for our return home. Leaving my lover at the airport was the hard part; going back home was easy. My husband was clueless; I pulled it off, now back to reality. Reality sucks!"

Adding some truth to the mix of lies gave Carissa as well as her husband a certain comfort level. Having her husband's blessings while away from home was significant for her mindset and time spent with her lover.

How you arrange your rendezvous together is your affair; the risks are high and so are the stakes. Each affair is your own, and you can take it to whatever heights you feel comfortable. There are definite drawbacks, and having an already suspecting partner can make it extremely difficult to put together. Would your partner, suspecting or not, be the type to want to surprise you or catch you cheating and show up at your hotel? That's something only you know and a chance you alone will take.

METHODOLOGY

- ♦ Whether you are driving or flying to your destination, go it alone. Meet up with your lover at the hotel. As nice as it may seem to travel with your lover, we don't need another movie made about how we got caught. Drive alone, fly alone, check-in alone. An innocent fender bender could put you at a place and time that's not explainable.

- ♦ Book separate rooms even though you will be sleeping in one. It's a small price to pay when your partner calls the hotel in which you are a registered guest. It really helps to have the hotel operator connect your partner to your room. Even if you don't answer the call when it comes in, you can check for messages and call your partner back from the privacy of your own room.

- ♦ Calling from the area code you are visiting is essential should your partner look at caller ID or dial *69.

- ♦ You must have your cell phone on at all times and be reachable in case of emergencies. Make sure you return your partner's call within an hour of the voice message. This limits worry on your partner's end and also reinforces that you are not "too tied up" (even if you are) to call back so expeditiously. Return your partner's call without your lover being present. Your apprehension in conversation will alert your partner to change.

♦ You and your lover must accept the initial ground rules to being in paradise together, and communication with your partner is a prerequisite.

Hats are off to you if you planned your excursion and pulled it off without a hitch. It may be easier for some and impossible for others, but regardless of the category you fall in, it's not without consequence.

CHAPTER 8

PUBLIC PLACES ...
DO WE DARE?

This isn't the type of chance you take when you buy a raffle, but it is one of the most common ways of getting caught.

They say, "The greatest risk in life is not taking one," but you have to ask yourself, "Is this the time?" You never know who knows whom, and do we really remember everyone who remembers meeting us?

When I say public places, I mean any place under the sun or moon that has more than the two of you present. This is a very gray area and completely a judgment call on your part as to whether you feel comfortable enough to venture out with someone other than your partner.

There are plenty of good explanations for being out with someone, be it a restaurant or even a bar, but there are a lot of public places that are hard to explain—e. g., beach, park, department store, hotel lobby. If you are part of white-bread corporate America, then perhaps a business lunch or dinner would suffice as an explanation. If you are part of the domestic god or goddess domain, a business lunch isn't going to float your partner's boat. What would you say if you were seen?

How do you explain the obvious exchange of affection, such as a small kiss or stroke of the hand, in the context of business? Maybe monkey business, but do you think people are blind or just pretend to be? Do you really think you can sit at a table or bar with your lover without touching?

As good as we would like to think we are, we haven't won the Oscar for any awards. We get caught up in the moment with our lover, and we become our own worst enemy. We all lose sight of reality at times, but being out in public with your lover isn't the place to lose sight of the consequences of being caught.

It's written all over our faces, and don't forget body language. All we need is someone to see any or all of this, and depending on how many channels it takes to get back to your partner, the story will be portrayed the way it was perceived and then some.

Should you be the daring type and plan a public outing with your lover, make sure you have a believable explanation in place should this meeting somehow get back to your partner. A quick, thought-out response is more readily accepted than a story made up on the spur of the moment that includes a lot of hesitation.

You know your partner better than anyone; you also know the circumstances and events that surround your life. Only you know what your partner can justify as an acceptable explanation. Most partners want to believe that an event such as "cheating" or "betrayal" is not true, and that the person telling all was wrong in his or her assumption. You could also get lucky if the "denial" factor kicks in, and your partner wants to believe *you* instead of someone who could drive a wedge between the two of you.

A line that I love and have always included in my conversations with my partner is "Believe nothing of what you hear and only half of what you see ... Believe nothing of what others see!"

Have the answer ready before the question is presented to you.

Jeanne, a thirty-five-year-old paralegal from Scranton, PA, describes her very close encounter, emotions, and suggestions.

"I remember picking out a small pub just outside of town, convenient in proximity, for a clandestine rendezvous. Sight unseen, it seemed out of the way, unknown, just safe. I suggested my lover and I meet for a drink after work. After meeting there once, twice, three times, I began to find a

comfort level with the pub. I never saw anyone who remotely looked familiar so I let my guard down and got caught up in a couple of moments of displayed affection. I couldn't find a balance with being so intimate behind closed doors and so platonic in public. I wanted to feel a sense of normalcy in our relationship even in those brief public moments."

"Approximately three months later, I received a phone call at work from my husband asking me if I ever heard of this small pub just outside of town. Being a quick thinker and aware that my husband couldn't possibly have known about this place, I immediately sensed suspicion."

"My heart was palpitating, I began to sweat but tried to remain calm and not surprised at this wonderful question. I was being confronted with my biggest fear and wasn't sure what was coming next."

"Had my husband presented me with this wonderful revelation off-guard and in person, there would have been no dancing around it. Stuttering, the look of shock, and body language (not the affectionate kind) would have left me open for more questioning. I obviously didn't have a pre-planned explanation in place and wouldn't

have had the same type of leverage that I had via 'ma bell.'

"As luck would have it, a frequent patron of the bar was also an acquaintance of my husband; and as luck would have it again, he bumped into my husband in a chance meeting. As I'm sure you can guess the next sentence, this acquaintance, who recognized me from sight, proceeded to tell my husband that he saw me having a drink with someone at this establishment."

"At first, my thoughts were all over the place: 'What else was seen?' 'How many times did he see me?' 'I'm caught!' 'How do I get out of this one?' 'I know, mistaken identity. No, that won't work.' 'Tell the truth! No, I'll never be trusted again.' 'How do I explain the kiss, the touching, the obvious that can't be covered by a hundred lies?'

"I knew I had to answer quickly and without hesitation! I promptly replied that I had gone to this bar for happy hour several times with various co-workers and had no idea to which this person was referring. It was all I could think of saying without an uncertain tone in my voice."

"I waited for the next sentence (I don't think I was breathing at this point), but there was none. My

husband didn't know anything more. I wouldn't have had a suitable explanation for the obvious displays of affection had it been told, and the happy hour story would have gone down with the Titanic."

"My husband's friend must have seen me having drinks that one time. Or perhaps saved my husband the embarrassment of telling all. Is this going to come back to bite me in the butt? Perhaps in their next chance meeting?"

"Suffice it to say, my lover and I never went back to that unknown, out-of-the-way, safe little pub again. For the next few months, we took our affair to a lower level and met in empty parking lots. As I can recall, happy hour was sometimes a lot happier and safer in the car."

Jeanne was lucky that her husband's friend didn't see or reveal the obvious displays of affection that she shared openly with her lover. It would have been her word against his; however, even if Jeanne were able to convince her husband to come over to her side, doubt would remain.

CHAPTER 9

Timing/Scheduling ...
Ticktock, Ticktock

Some people believe in seizing the moment; others believe it's the quality of time and not the quantity. What do you believe?

Timing and scheduling is one of the hardest juggling acts I've ever encountered in an affair. Time with your lover, time with your family, and never the two should meet—juggling time between the two needs to be scheduled effectively as well as discreetly. Time at home, or lack of time thereof, should never go noticed by your partner. The time you've always invested at home shouldn't change because you'd rather be in a better sexual place. Your absence is not going to make your partner's heart grow fonder, but make him or her ponder as to your whereabouts.

It's difficult to outline just how you should schedule your time between your lover and your partner because you are the only one who knows the details of your life. I can, however, share with you the research I have gathered from other jugglers who have become excellent adulterers.

Most of us think that juggling time during the course of the workday is not an option when having an affair. We're obviously getting paid to work, have a job to do, and have a responsibility to our employer to either get the work done, or be done. So how is it that we can work in an affair throughout the course of the workday? It's not as hard as it may sound and does take some planning, but the elimination of doubt in our partners is far more important. In this genre, time is not abundant but can be gratifying.

Depending on your occupation, my first recommendation is to plan time either before work, during an extended lunch, or following an early dismissal. This of course is contingent on your lover being available and/or able to meet you during the same timeframes.

THE WORKING PERSON

There are numerous explanations for getting to work an hour or two later in the morning and are more readily accepted by your partner. These explanations should be brief, simple, to the point, and explained to your employer prior and to your partner after, if necessary.

Additional time during an extended lunch gets a unanimous vote for time manipulation. Again, give a quick explanation to your employer for the extended time, and perhaps no explanation is necessary to your partner. Should your partner try to contact you during lunch, time is easily explainable with a simple excuse of a "long line in the bank, running a few errands, left my cell phone in the car, business lunch, shopping, etc." As long as your partner can reach you back at home or at work in the afternoon, those long errands during lunch shouldn't be questioned or suspicious.

Elizabeth, a fifty-two-year-old store manager from Edwards, Colorado, tells how time with her lover began with coffee, tea, or me in the morning.

"Meeting at the coffee shop or motel for a quick good morning wake-up call was workable between the two of us. An early morning meeting or errands before work was my excuse of choice to my partner if I needed one; otherwise, nothing was necessary to explain."

The morning hours are usually the busiest time of day for most of us. By the time your partner gets situated at work, home, getting the kids off to school, errands, whatever your situation, you could have already spent at least a couple of hours with your lover without any suspicion or phone calls. There are always emergencies or the "I forgot something" phone call, so make sure you still have this window of opportunity covered and your cell phone turned on. Being available and easily accessible 24/7 is the key factor in doubt elimination.

As I mentioned above, lunch hours were extremely filling to most disloyal spouses, not to mention satisfying. Manipulating or creating additional time during lunch is more practical than coming in late or leaving early without a good explanation to your employer; it also doesn't raise as many eyebrows in the workplace. Don't forget that your partner, in all probability, is still involved in his or her own busy day and is less likely to look for you.

Rachel, a forty-six-year-old executive assistant from Detroit, Michigan, always leaves her cell phone in the car should her husband look for her during those promiscuous hours.

"It allowed me uninterrupted time with my lover, and I was always able to return my partner's call within a reasonable, unsuspicious amount of time."

Should you choose to receive an interruption while with your lover, take the call outside (even if you have to get up and dressed to do it). Believe it or not, the tone of your voice and your lack of *freedom of speech* could arouse suspicion as to where you are and what you might be doing. This also prevents breaking the mood with your lover, who may in turn become uneasy in hearing your conversation with your partner. Remember, an affair is all about those wonderful, hard-to-find, stolen moments; don't lose them before they begin and don't lose your partner over a slip of the tongue.

Needless to say, all the above isn't workable if your lover works or lives a fair distance from a common meeting place; therefore, time before, during, or after work won't work, unless one of you is from the household of the ...

DOMESTIC GOD OR GODDESS DOMAIN

I think it's safe to assume that in today's day and age at least one member of your household has a full-time job, unless of course you were born with a silver spoon in your mouth and can sit poolside all day without financial worries.

If you are the one at home, then your time may or may not be more flexible than the working person.

Most stay-at-home moms or dads are home for one reason: family. Depending on the ages of your children, juggling time during your partner's workday may not be as easy or difficult as you may think. Of course, if your children are of school age, you are ahead of the game. You and your lover can easily plan time together throughout the course of the day because your time is flexible and can be worked into your lover's window of opportunity. Assuming you drive the kids to the bus stop or school, you can now spend a couple of hours with your lover. If the morning isn't feasible, then lunch works as long as you are back in time to maintain your responsibilities at home and eliminate suspicion from your partner.

Should you choose to have an affair with young children under school age, then juggling time is going to be much more difficult. This scenario requires a baby sitter or family member to mind the kids while you're out with your lover. This now involves putting others on a need-to-know basis, in addition to letting your partner know who's minding the store. If your partner is unsuspecting, then going out for a few hours may not raise any eyebrows; however, this should be limited to once a week and not on a consistent basis.

An interesting comment made by someone who preferred to remain anonymous : *"Prior* *to my partner's suspicions, I would plan time with my lover in the evening while my partner watched our young children. This may sound morally incorrect, but then again was there ever a time my affair was correct? What I was doing wasn't going to be well received by my partner even if someone else was babysitting."*

"Ironically, I knew where my partner was for the evening."

CHAPTER 10

INTERNET AFFAIRS ...
CLICK, DOUBLE CLICK

I can remember a time when a mouse was a gray furry creature that gave me the creeps and hopes of never crossing paths again. Today, we can't live without a mouse, wireless or otherwise. Just a couple of clicks and we're on our way to potentially having an affair via the Internet.

The use of the Internet and the available meeting sites has definitely caused infidelity to climb at an all-time high statistical rate. The ease of access in meeting people from the confines of our own home or office has certainly opened many doors to infidelity. We go through them because they're there, we're curious, and, as one of our leaders said, "because we can."

Times have certainly changed (especially in politics) and so have extramarital affairs, at least the way they now begin. I call it "reverse meeting." The computer age is constantly evolving, introducing us to new and exciting meeting sites where foreplay and cybersex now exist in chat rooms and emails.

Most of my research on Internet affairs was done on various sites in a category that was defined as "not so happily married." For obvious reasons, it isn't safe to post a photo to your profile, and your profile should have as much truth to it without making you identifiable. Your profile is what attracts others in similar situations who are also curious or looking for a prospective lover.

As I've said so many times before, your reasons for having, wanting, or thinking about an affair are your own; where and how you meet your lover is at your discretion.

Most married couples are not at liberty to venture out to bars or restaurants on a consistent basis to enable them to meet people. But what about the selection process? Do we really want to meet someone who may be looking to fall in love? *"Pardon me, are you interested in having an affair?"*

The infamous World Wide Web has done the sorting for us and brings us together on a common platform with common interests and provides the common ground we need to explore. As easy as this might seem, it's also not without risk.

Note: Many couples have been caught cheating because they are computer illiterate and have failed to erase their history.

Some very important protocol to follow before traveling down the information super highway to the World Wide Web:

♦ Never use a computer shared by your partner, children, and/or other members of your household. If you only have one home shared computer, then you must be very careful to erase the sites you've visited.

♦ Delete your history by clicking on the tools icon on Internet Explorer, then click on Internet Options. On the General tab, go down to Temporary Internet Files and click on "delete files" (check box for online content as well) and "delete cookies"; this will delete all pages viewed on the Internet.

♦ Right below Temporary Internet Files is History. Click on "clear history"; this will clear the links to the pages you just viewed on the Internet. Set your "days to keep pages in history" to zero.

♦ Using a shared computer with your partner can also leave you open to unsuspecting software that may be installed on your computer. There are many different types and brands of spyware software that do just that, "spy." They can capture and memorize your keystrokes so that your partner can easily read Web sites visited even though you deleted them. It also reads your screen name(s) and passwords, which can easily lead your partner to your various email accounts. (Refer to Chapter 4 on email.)

♦ If you use your own private and personal laptop or notebook, don't think you're home free. Make sure it's password protected through the Windows start-up screen and delete everything; there should be no comfort levels when it comes to infidelity.

♦ Depending on your occupation, your office computer may not be the likely choice either. If you use your work-based computer, chances are you may be monitored in some way by the technology services department. Check to see what rules are in place regarding allowed and banned sites. As long as you are discreet and do not abuse the system, you should be fine. After all, how much time can we spend surfing the Internet for a romantic interlude without our MIS department noticing how productive we've become in the "chat" room instead of the boardroom?

Security is more about common sense than computer literacy. If you are worried that you may be caught, chances are you are not using your toolbars correctly.

CHAPTER 11

Lust vs. Love ...
When the Smoke Clears

I can see the forest through the trees, or is it the trees through the forest?

They say the mind can play tricks on us, but what about the heart? What happens when the mind and heart are in sync and playing tricks together? Where does that leave us? Whatever the reason for the affair, the effect infidelity has on a relationship is devastating.

I have seen many marriages and relationships end because lustful feelings are mistaken for the wonderful, magical feeling of love. Think you've found your soul mate, the love of your life, and your reason for living again? Well, guess again. How do you know you're not caught up in feelings of lust and not love? Gentlemen, don't let the little head rule the big head, and ladies, there's no such thing as Prince Charming or his white horse. Reality must be present at all times.

While in a marriage or relationship that is obviously lacking something, we look to fulfill our needs through someone else. Whether it is intentional or accidental, what we do realize is that we don't consciously want to hurt anyone. We want to somehow recapture what we seem to be lacking with our partners. In our minds, we believe that if we get involved in an affair, it will be pure, unadulterated bang-off-the-wall sex, along with the mental stimulation that appears to be long gone. What else could it possibly be? We're married or committed to a relationship, perhaps with children, we love our spouses, still feeling a sense of obligation, respect and loyalty, so how could we fall in love? Impossible! We go into the affair with a particular mindset and sometimes end up with quite another.

The newness of a relationship, the passion, the butterflies, the "I can't wait until the next time" scenario all create wonderful emotions that put the spring back in our step. Our thoughts constantly gravitate toward the last memory together. ∞The anticipation of the next lovemaking session. ∞The tingling sensation that gets our juices flowing and consumes our bodies with every thought of the earth moving and the angels singing. ∞Weakness in the knees. ∞The touch. ∞The kiss. ∞The compatibility and mental stimulation. Did I leave anything out? Why wouldn't we think all these wonderful feelings aren't love? They don't exist with our partners anymore, but are very much alive with our lovers.

The heart is an extremely susceptible organ when our physical and/or emotional needs haven't been met through the life and relationship we share with our partner. We become vulnerable to all the above-described emotions, and we embrace the opportunity to feel so alive. It's food for our soul and a great ego booster to know that someone other than our partner thinks we're all that and a bag of chips!

You know yourself better than anyone, and you alone know what you feel in your heart. I'm not a connoisseur on love, and I'm not here to tell you that what you feel isn't genuine. But before you commence divorce proceedings for your newfound love, there are several important issues you need to realize.

Think back to the time you were able to have an open, honest relationship that led you to your commitment with your partner. Most of us thought it was love or we wouldn't have committed. Time spent together was extensive and easy to come by. You were able to explore a lot about each other in a short amount of time. The getting-to-know-you stage was easy. We were able to walk openly and freely everywhere our hearts desired. None of this is possible in an affair, unless you want to get caught (and if you did, you wouldn't be reading this book).

Reflect on the time spent with your lover, quality versus quantity. If you think you've fallen in love and are seriously considering leaving your partner, then you need to invest in the quantity of time. How well do you know this person outside of the fun and games you've been sharing? A day here, an hour there, do you think it's enough to disrupt the life you have for a life you think you'll have? Fantasy versus reality, how we write the script in our minds doesn't always come out that way in the real world.

Eric, a forty-two-year-old accountant from Boston, Massachusetts, shares his distinctions between lust and love.

"I remember my first affair. I wasn't consciously looking to have an affair when I found myself extremely attracted to another woman. I unexpectedly met someone, and she then consumed my every thought. What was this feeling? I'm married, with children; I'm supposed to feel this way about my wife, no one else. Well, tell it to my heart. It took over hook, line, and sinker. I was in love, and no one was going to tell me differently."

"What time I could sneak away from my then-unsuspecting wife, I did. Time spent was more than wonderful, and every moment apart seemed like days. One year into this affair, I realized that I could no longer live with one person and be in love

with another. Convinced of my feelings, I left my family to be with my lover. I never admitted the real reason for leaving; I just blamed it on everything else that was lacking from our marriage."

"For the first few months, I was on cloud nine being able to spend so much time with my lover and do more of the things I couldn't do while living with my wife. As the months went on, I started to see my lover for her true person. I slowly began to feel all those wonderful emotions slip away and then realized what a mistake I made. I allowed lust to consume my emotions and fool me into believing it was love. The theory that "things are not always as they seem" hit like a ton of bricks. The smoke cleared."

In hindsight, Eric should have given his affair more time by keeping it as an affair. I believe he would have seen his lover for the person she was and not the fantasy he created in his mind. An affair is just that, a fantasy of newfound emotions that spark our interest and consume our hearts. It often mimics love and takes on a form of its own.

Staying true to reality is key to knowing lust versus love. We come full circle in our not-so-perfect world by having an affair. It's sometimes the reason why we are able to remain in our marriage or relationship for so many years. We have our spouse, our family, our work, and our lover. Our lives and hearts are full. End of story.

Three important things to remember:

- ♦ Don't lose sight of reality by those lustful feelings.
- ♦ Invest the time in an affair as an affair.
- ♦ Try to get to know your lover for the true person they are and endearing qualities that he or she "seems" to possess.

In the end, Eric went back to his wife. They do put erasers on pencils; does your partner have a big enough eraser?

EPILOGUE

It's exhausting to think that we need to pay so much attention to detail before getting involved in an extramarital affair. However, the bigger question remains - do we want to get caught?

As I said in my Introduction, nothing is fool proof or guaranteed. Even if you've memorized every chapter in this book, it doesn't preclude you from making an error. Your partner and the details of your life should be the main components in your current extramarital relationship. This book cannot eliminate doubt or suspicions in your partner, nor does it outline the type of affair you should have based on your life. The contents of this book, combined with your sense and sensibilities, will help you to avoid the many mishaps and foolish mistakes that many will make when it comes to infidelity. It's designed to give your affair a longer shelf life.

All the people who were willing to share their stories and experiences with me had the same view; they were eager to help others learn from their mistakes. Although there were many different views being brought to the table of deception and betrayal, the bottom line was the same for each and every contributor; not one wanted to get caught, and not one wanted to hurt his or her family.

They all, however, wished overwhelmingly that they had read this book before embarking upon their affairs.